Referencing, copying and adaptation are all around us, however our need for authenticity and uniqueness is bigger than ever. No matter where you look, we are surrounded by all kinds of great ideas. Yet when we do our work, most of us ignore them. Instead, our egos force us to re-invent the wheel, over and over again. As if we want to state: 'it's only ME that came up with all of this. I thought of this, and no one else.'

However, if there is a perfectly fine wheel available, why would you put all that time and effort in reinventing it again? There are so many great ideas already there, just waiting to be used.

'Same, Same But Different' challenges the taboo of using the same idea twice. Over 3 years, Max Siedentopf sent a series of ideas in the shape of drawings and short descriptions to over 50 international photographers to quite literally photograph the same idea.

In our constant hunt for unique ideas and authenticity, we often forget that execution matters just the same. Maybe even more.

'Same, Same But Different' illustrates that having the same starting point (an idea) actually emphasizes the artist's own interpretation in the various end results.

So let's be open to both new and old ideas, because if you look hard enough you'll find that everything has been done before. Don't let that discourage you!

The idea is just the start.

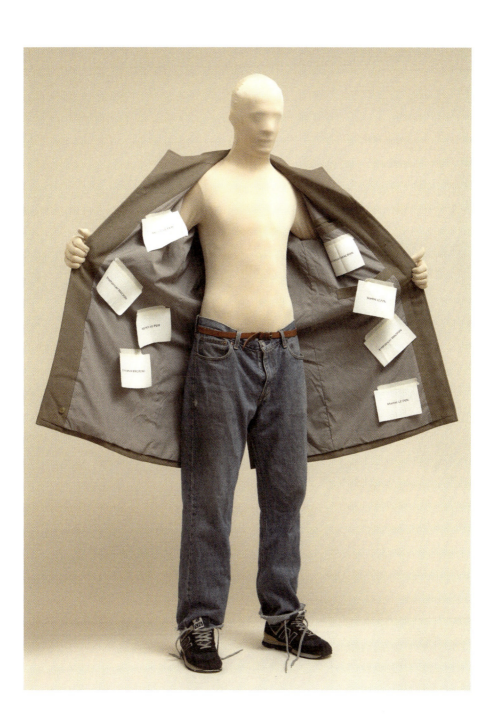

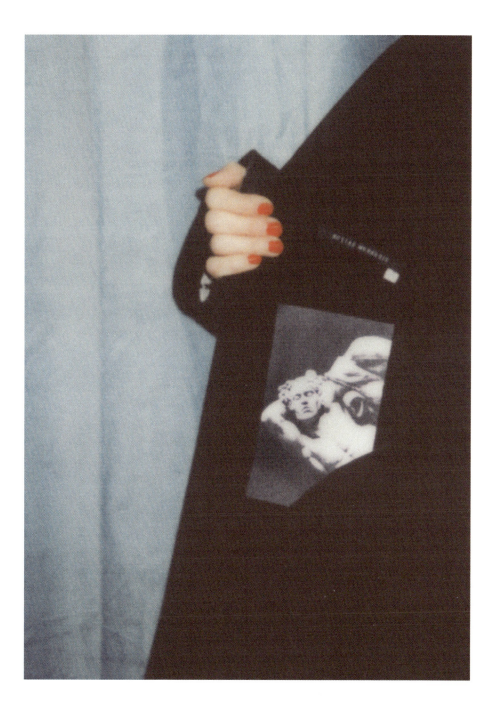

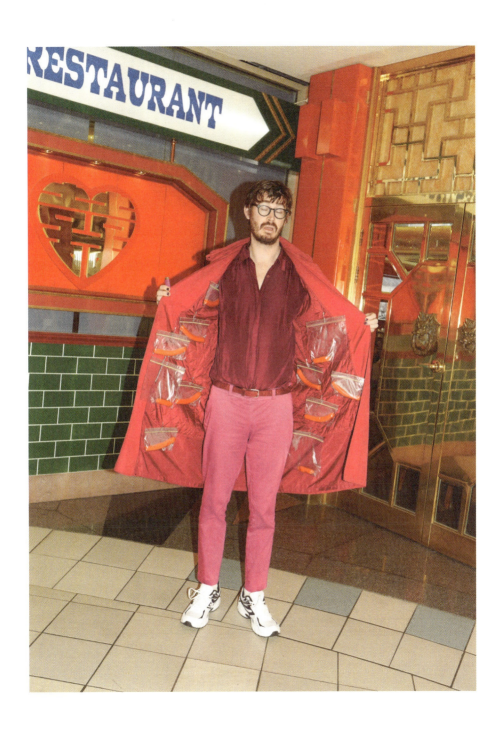

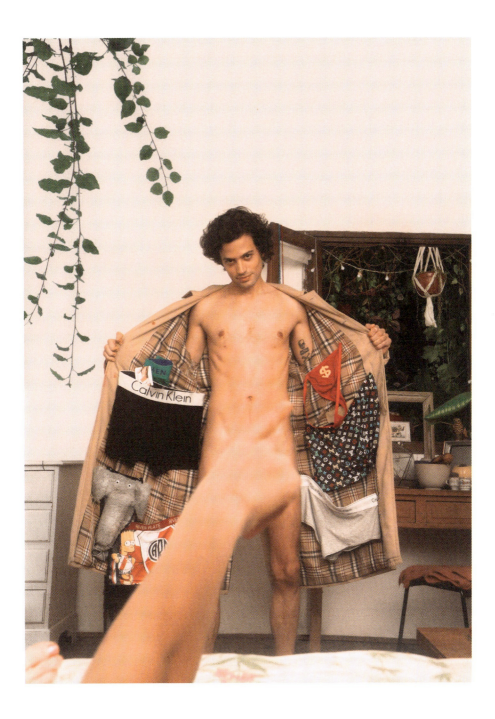

lukas korshan

peggy kuiper

jp bonino

jo duck

lena & zoe

annie collinge

luke stephenson

romain sellier

anouk van kalmthout

michiel meewis

sarah blais

andrea artemisio

kelia anne maccluskey

a middle aged
man cries
while he
strokes
a cat

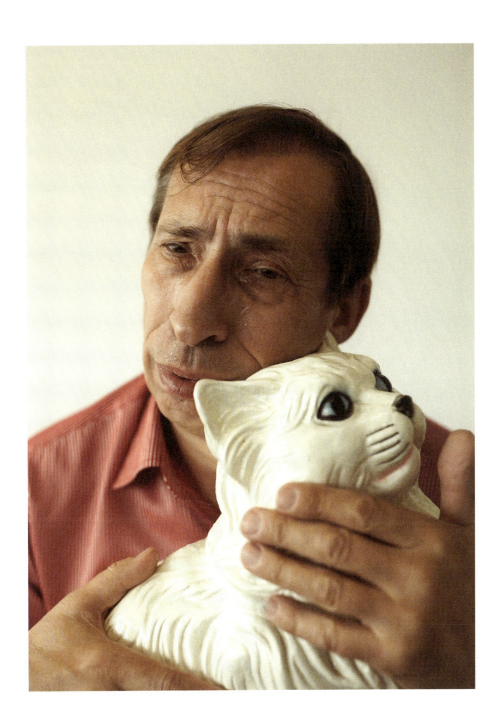

parker day

francesco nazardo

michiel meewis

annie collinge

jp bonino

jo duck

trisha ward

luke stephenson

boris camaca

andrea artemisio

imke ligthart

romain sellier   peggy kuiper

a woman bleeds out of her nose. she holds a bottle of ketchup.

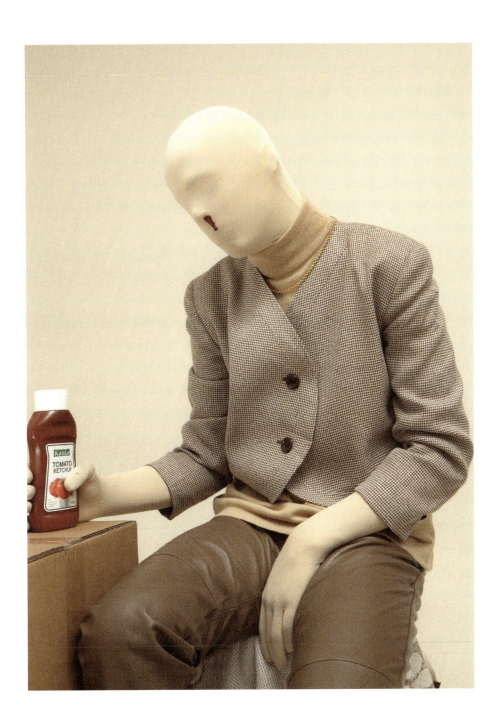

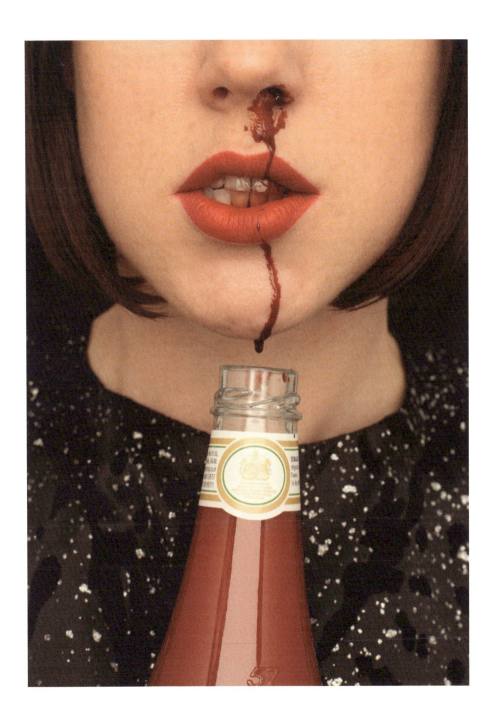

julia et vincent

peggy kuiper

kelia anne maccluskey

jack buster

luke stephenson

chris schoonover

romain sellier

annie collinge

paul rousteau

jo duck

michiel meewis

parker day

andrea artemisio

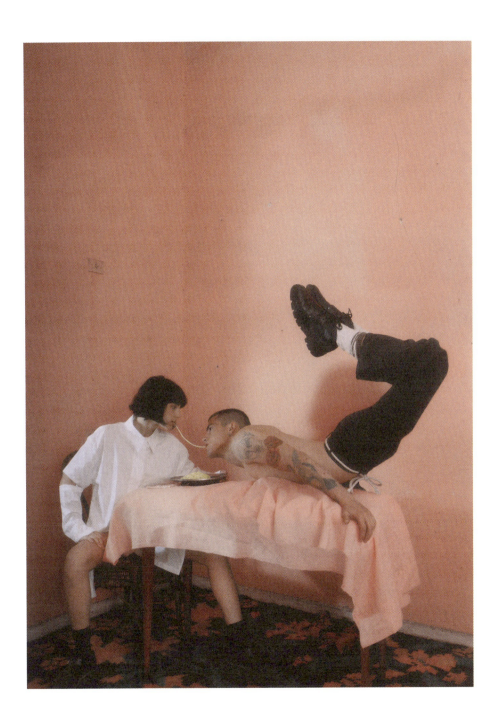

luke stephenson

barrie hullegie

jo duck

michiel meewis

jack buster

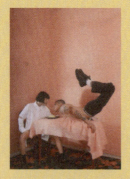

jp bonino

dham srifuengfung

annie collinge

elizabeth gabrielle lee

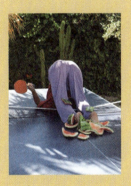

imke ligthart

dima hohlov

andrea artemisio

emmie america

a man stands and looks at his wrist to check the time. He doesn't notice that ~~is~~ instead of a watch, there is a sausage around his arm.

lukas korshan

michiel meewis

clifford jago

vo duck

marloes haarmans

anouk van kalmthout

romain sellier

paul rousteau

dham srifuengfung

andrea artemisio

jan hoek

luke stephenson

olesya asanova

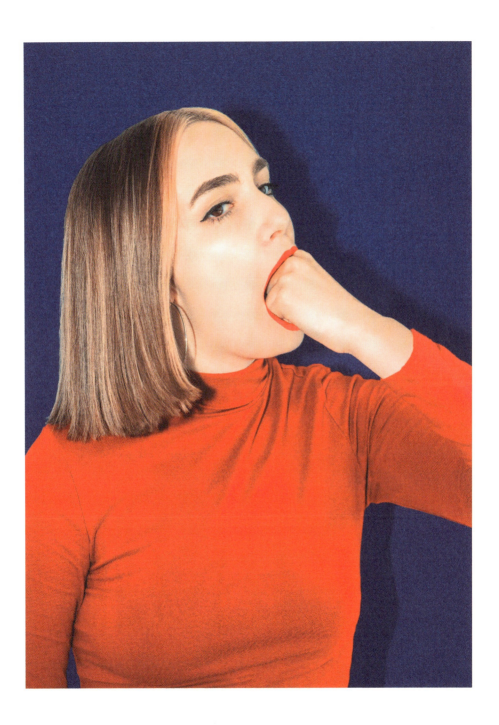

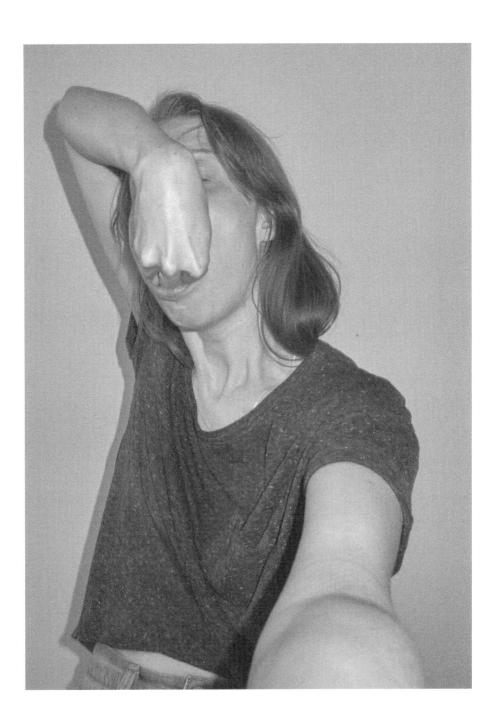

kelia anne macclushey

romain sellier

michiel meewis

parker day

luke stephenson

jo duck

paul rousteau

annie collinge

andrea artemisio

imke ligthart

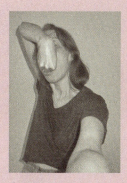
trisha ward

peter puklus

barrie hullegie

a handshake.
one of the hands is a foot.

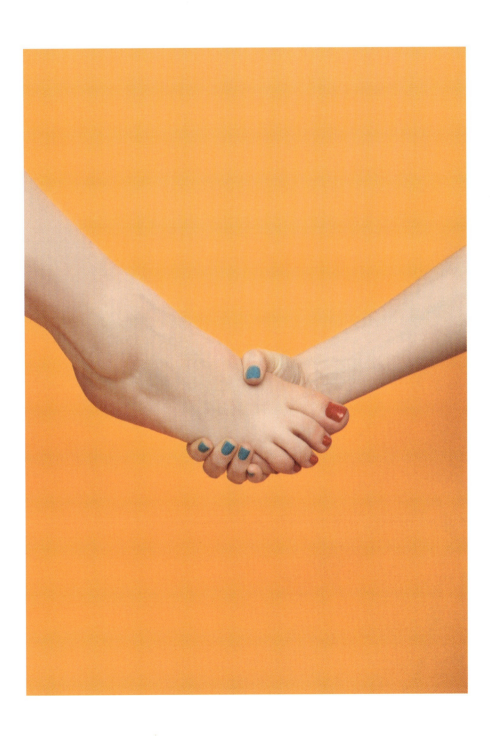

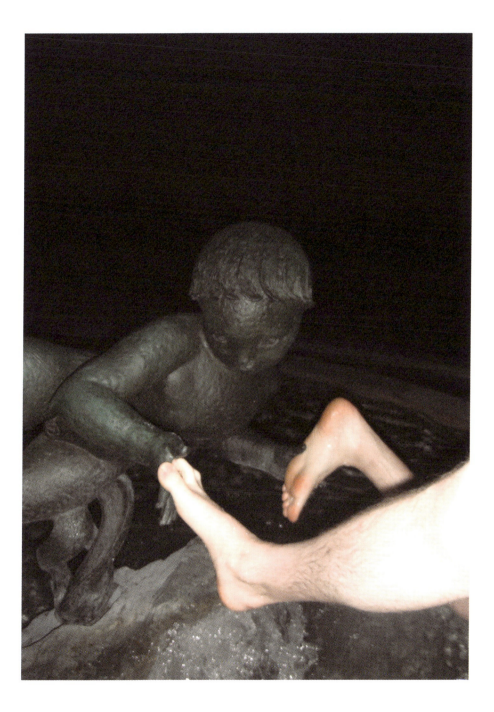

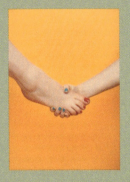

luke stephenson

kelia anne maccluskey

jo duck

jennifer cheng

michiel meewis

andrea artemisio

romain sellier

caroline tompkins

jp bonino

eamonn freel

imke ligthart

peter puklus

henry gorse

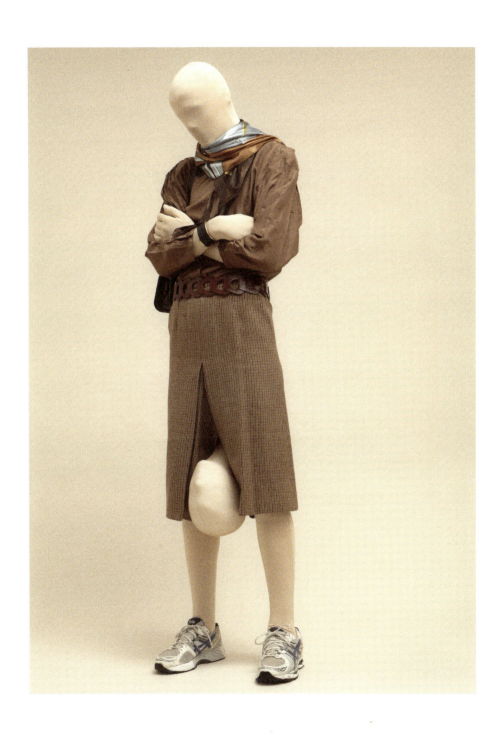

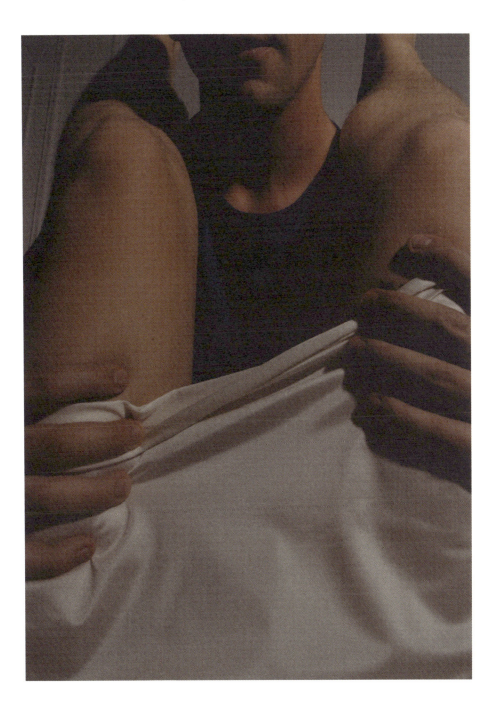

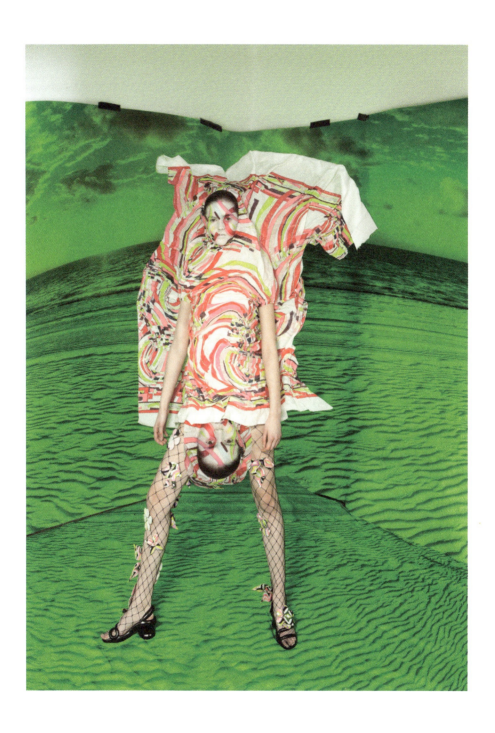

luke stephenson

jp bonino

arielle bobb-willis

peggy kuiper

romain sellier

andrea artemisio

michiel meewis

tom blesch

imke ligthart

reece+dean

brian galderisi

caroline tompkins

jo duck

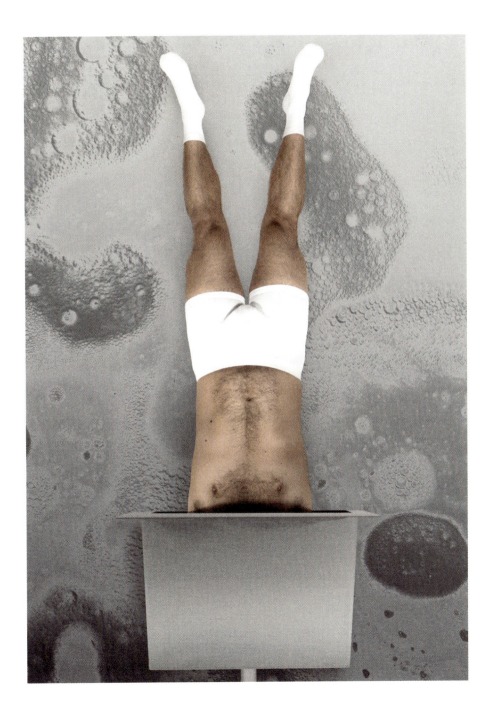

maxwell granger

david avazzadeh

peggy kuiper

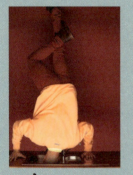
luke stephenson

jo duck

ruinez

eamonn freel

annie collinge

henry gorse

michiel meewis

jp bonino

marloes haarmans

andrea artemisio

luke stephenson

romain sellier

olesya asanova

jo duck

peggy kuiper

jp bonino

jack buster

paul rousteau

david arazzadeh

michiel meewis

sebastian henkel

andrea artemisio

dham srifuengfung

luke stephenson

lucy alex mac

david arazzadeh

olesya asanova

scandebergs

kelia anne maccluskey

paul rousteau

peter puklus

dham srifuengfung

romain sellier

michiel meewis

andrea artemisio

jo duck

luke stephenson

jp bonino

reece + dean

annie collinge

dham srifuengfung

olesya asanova

ruinez

romain sellier

jo duck

sanja marusic

michiel meewis

dexter lander

andrea artemisio

SAME, SAME BUT DIFFERENT
Concept by Max Siedentopf

Photographs by
Andrea Artemisio, Annie Collinge, Anouk Van Kalmthout, Arielle Bobb-Willis,
Barrie Hullegie, Brian Galderisi, Boris Camaca, Caroline Tompkins, Chris Schoonover,
Clifford Jago, David Avazzadeh, Dexter Lander, Dham Srifuengfung, Dima Hohlov,
Eamonn Freel, Elizabeth Gabrielle Lee, Emmie America, Francesco Nazardo, Henry Gorse,
Imke Ligthart, Jack Buster, Jan Hoek, Jennifer Cheng, Jo Duck, Jp Bonino, Julia Et Vincent,
Kelia Anne MacCluskey, Lena & Zoe, Lucy Alex Mac, Lukas Korschan, Luke Stephenson,
Marloes Haarmans, Maxwell Granger, Michiel Meewis, Olesya Asanova, Parker Day,
Paul Rousteau, Peggy Kuiper, Peter Puklus, Reece + Dean, Romain Sellier, Ruinez,
Sanja Marusic, Sarah Blais, Scandebergs, Sebastian Henkel, Trisha Ward

Many thanks to
Vanessa Deutsch, Lancelot Prat, Didi the cat, Lea & Maria, Sally Anne Bolton,
Julia Dias, Fuchs, Opa Herrmann, Abby Bennett, Marawa The Amazing, Luke Perillo,
Paul Miller, Richie 1250, Benjamin Hancock, Colette Miller, Simone Paige Jones,
Christina Dietze, Asli, Bronte Sommerfeld, Munib Alihromic, Dr McDreamy,
Luke Rush, Radar Rad, Jordan Drysdale, Morag Mason, Duval Agency, Bec Martin,
Chelsea Bagan, Trophy Wife, Jebediah, Xeneb, Eckhard & Dietlind Siedentopf

First edition published by HYENA, London, UK
© 2020 HYENA for this edition
©2020 Max Siedentopf for concept, drawings and texts
©2020 referenced photographers for photographs

HYENA
hyena-editions.com
ISBN 978-1-9163707-0-8